engaging EXPERTS

Your Guide to the People and Connections you Need to Go from Ordinary to Extraordinary

A Compilation by Cathy L. Davis

ENGAGING EXPERTS
Your Guide to the People and Connections You Need to Go from Ordinary to Extraordinary
UpsiDaisy Press

Published by **UpsiDaisy Press**, St. Louis, MO
Copyright ©2021 Cathy L. Davis
All rights reserved.

No part of this publication may be reproduced, stored in a retrieval system, or transmitted in any form or by any means, electronic, mechanical, photocopying, recording, scanning, or otherwise, except as permitted under Section 107 or 108 of the 1976 United States Copyright Act, without the prior written permission of the Publisher. Requests to the Publisher for permission should be addressed to Office@daviscreative.com, please put **Engaging Experts** in the subject line.

Limit of Liability/Disclaimer of Warranty: While the publisher and author have used their best efforts in preparing this book, they make no representations or warranties with respect to the accuracy or completeness of the contents of this book and specifically disclaim any implied warranties of merchantability or fitness for a particular purpose. No warranty may be created or extended by sales representatives or written sales materials. The advice and strategies contained herein may not be suitable for your situation. You should consult with a professional where appropriate. Neither the publisher nor author shall be liable for any loss of profit or any other commercial damages, including but not limited to special, incidental, consequential, or other damages.

All contributing authors to this anthology have submitted their chapters to an editing process, and have accepted the recommendations of the editors at their own discretion. All authors have approved their chapters prior to publication.

Cover and Interior Design: Davis Creative, DavisCreative.com
Writing Coach and Editor: Kay Uhles, KayClarkUhles.com

Compilation by Cathy Davis
Engaging Experts: Your Guide to the People and Connections You Need to Go from Ordinary to Extraordinary

ISBN: 978-1-7347971-3-8 (paperback)
       978-1-7347971-6-9 (ebook)

2020

091021

TABLE OF CONTENTS

Cathy Davis
How to Spot an Engaging Expert 1

Rebecca Hall Gruyter
Staying Visible During Challenging Times 5

Connie Whitman
From Unknown to Number One 11

Kelly Nagle
The Journey from Rock Bottom 17

Julie Hood
Five Steps to Course Creation 23

Dr. Maurya D. Cockrell
The SDoH Solutionary 29

Cindy Rowan
Leadership Development: From Myths to Impact 35

Deb Gaut
Big, Bold, Audacious Change 41

Trish Hall
Art of Living Spiritually 47

Dr. Glenn T. Miller
Ace of All Trades 53

Rob Whitman
For Sale by Owner 59

Kimberly Weitkamp
Avoiding Marketing Free Fall 65

Joanne Weiland
Go for the Green 71

Meredith McVehil
Sleepless to Hopeful about Money 77

CATHY DAVIS

How to Spot an Engaging Expert

When you are considering making a change in your personal life or in your business, you quite often turn to an expert to help you make that happen. We have all been through quite a few changes during this past year (2020); and perhaps, like me, you reached out to at least one new expert to help you navigate your next best steps.

I started 2020 with the goal of up-leveling my financial services support. Even prior to the pandemic, I was on the hunt for a new bookkeeper, a new CPA, and was even considering changing banks. As we moved into a Spring 2020 quarantine, I elevated my hunt to my number one priority, reaching out for referrals and recommendations, and scheduling phone interviews. Although it took much longer than I expected, I eventually narrowed down my options and have moved forward with transitioning my business finances to new support staff.

I learned a lot about looking for the experts I needed—there's much more to being an expert than merely claiming the title and "hanging out a shingle." An *Engaging Expert* brings with them a combination of education, experience, enthusiasm, and what I call "community collateral."

*****

Education

Yes, it's great to have the schooling and the extra alphabet letters behind a name, but there is much more to being an expert than four-plus years of college. What I'm talking about here is book-smarts and people-smarts, as well as ongoing real-life education. What additional courses, credentials, or adult learning experiences have they acquired since college? Who have they trained or mentored with? Can they carry on a normal conversation without resorting to their industry jargon? Can they answer the questions I don't even know to ask?

In my exploration to find the financial support I wanted, I soon learned the trick was to find the Engaging Experts who could integrate their book-smarts with ongoing real-life experiences and more effectively help me reach my goals.

Experience

I hate technology—almost as much as I despise bookkeeping. I know enough about each to recognize I'd rather be doing something else. I was on a mission to delegate out these tasks to people who had much more experience with them than I did. How long have they been working in their area of expertise? What does their client base look like? Who endorses their work? I was looking for Engaging Experts who have spent years honing their craft and could apply it in creative ways to help me streamline our processes. I needed to be able to trust them to handle the finances, do the work correctly (to keep the IRS happy), and keep me apprised of what I needed to know.

Enthusiasm

Years ago, during my corporate years as a team leader for a group of creatives, I learned very quickly to only hire the happy campers. Happy attracts happy. Happy people exude excitement and enthusiasm about their topic of expertise and can usually talk non-stop about this "thing" they love. Their enthusiasm becomes the fuel of their existence and mirrors their commitment to sharing what they know. Engaging Experts don't *have to* do what they do, they *get to*—which is why I knew I was looking for new (happy) financial services experts who were excited and eager to help—and would enthusiastically make my life easier.

*****

Community Collateral

The first thing I did once I identified the type of experts I needed was to ask trusted colleagues for referrals. Discussing my needs with peers helped me to narrow down more precisely what I was looking for; that is, people who were highly respected by their peers and clients.

Street cred can be some of the best community collateral around. Experts who want to get noticed make sure they network with other experts and embed themselves in local and online communities. If someone was referred to me more than once, they got bumped to the top of my "Learn More" list. I soon had a credible short list of Engaging Experts who were highly regarded by their peers and viable candidates to help me grow our business.

These three traits—education, experience, and enthusiasm—along with community collateral—allowed me to identify the perfect experts I needed to meet my immediate needs.

*****

Engaging Experts, just like those found in this published collaboration, are willing to step up, stand out, and make a difference. Each one shines in their zone of expertise and is committed to helping you take your life and/or your business from ordinary to extraordinary.

No matter where you are in life or in business, these Engaging Experts are here to serve and enrich your day. Reach out (via the contact info and connection resources included in their bios at the end of each chapter). Each holds the magical combination of education, experience, enthusiasm, and community collateral you just might be looking for!

Continued...

Cathy Davis is founder/CEO of Davis Creative Publishing Partners. After a corporate career as a creative director at Bank of America Trust, Cathy struck out on her own in January of 2004. Originally offering branding and design Services, Cathy pivoted the company in support of authors in 2007. The Davis Creative Publishing Partners division now helps speakers, trainers, consultants, and experts use the power of publishing as a marketing tool to grow their businesses. Cathy's husband, Jack, joined the company in 2008 after almost 20 years at Fleishman-Hillard, a global public relations firm. Together, they now use their decades of experience as visual and verbal communicators to help their clients reap the benefits of publishing for both personal and business growth.

cathy@daviscreative.com
www.DavisCreative.com
www.linkedin.com/in/cathyldavis/
www.facebook.com/DavisCreativeLLC
www.youtube.com/channel/UC5L1yOYzT0gPP-tXY02ltVA
www.instagram.com/cathyl.davis/

REBECCA HALL GRUYTER

Staying Visible During Challenging Times

Those of you who've depended on public-speaking platforms to build your business may feel like the rug has been pulled out from under you (As an international speaker, I understand). Yes, the global pandemic has presented challenges—and new opportunities! It's time for speakers to get creative, versatile, and visible so they can continue to bring their messages forward—and be willing to bring them forward to reach the people who need it most.

Below are five ways to expand your visibility without speaking in person:

Embrace Virtual Platforms

Have you noticed that the places or events where you have appeared are switching to virtual events? Make that switch too by preparing yourself to become THE go-to online speaker! Because you're in closer focus on screen, get really intentional about your appearance, your voice, cadence, and volume. Frame your content so it's as engaging and concise as possible. Make sure your tech—camera, microphone, lighting, background (clear and clean)—are high-quality. Set up your online capabilities, get personalized backdrops; make sure they position you powerfully, intentionally, and professionally.

Hot Tip #1: The whole world needs to hear your message! Now you can apply for online speaking engagements all over the world, not just within travel distance. You can actually reach more people than being limited by who can make it to a specific location.

Hot Tip #2: Check out the "Speaker Talent Search" (link in bio) to apply for speaking and visibility opportunities. You don't have to do it all on your own. We facilitate the Speaker Talent Search several times a year as a way to give back to speakers so that they can expand their spheres of influence and reach more people with their messages.

Hot Tip #3: When you show up in these powerful virtual platforms, remember to treat them like you are on "stage." Show up authentically, powerfully, and professionally. Resist the urge to show up too casually; this can de-position you. (If you are not able to show up powerfully on video that day, then make sure to have a professional headshot that shows up on screen and keep your camera off.) If this is a casual support group, it is fine to show up more casually; however, be mindful, when you are showing up as the expert/speaker that you are showing up representing yourself in that manner.

Step into Leading Your Own Podcast

We know that about one-fourth of the U.S. population listens to podcasts every week and likely will continue beyond the pandemic[1]. Big benefits for you: Your listeners are seeking your message and tend to be highly engaged and loyal over time, so you can build wonderful connections and a high-quality list of ideal clients. What a wonderful way to transform more lives with your gifts. Plus, you can repurpose your content to build blogs, create books, and grow your list.

Hot Tip #4: As you create a collection of these blogs/content, you can create ebooks/summaries as downloadable resources that people can sign up for on your list to receive. If you cluster them together (25,000-40,000 words) you have enough content to bring forward as a book.

Hot Tip #5: If it feels too daunting to commit to leading a weekly show, then consider leading a summit or interview series. It doesn't have to be something you are signing up to do forever; it can be something you do for a period of time and/or on a particular subject. Make sure you have a way for people to sign up, follow you, and get on your list so you can continue the relationship beyond the interview series.

---

[1] PodcastHosting.org, In-Depth & Transparent Podcast Hosting Reviews, Last Updated: October 3, 2020, https://podcasthosting.org/podcast-statistics/?gclid=CjwKCAiAz4b_BRBbEiw A5XlVVm-56WtO2NorNXlV8993lN9xvGKDwhB0NLI1j4rNEPW07y47AKRdZGhoC-dQQAvD_BwE/

Consider Writing a Book

If you have a message lying on your heart or if people keep telling you, "You should write a book," now is the time to do it! I've heard from clients—and experienced myself—that publishing their books helped to generate more leads, close more deals, and get better speaking engagements (virtual or live). Especially when they were able to launch their books as best-sellers. This helps authors and their content be strategically positioned and more visible while they reach more people with their messages. These are all positive impacts for you and your business.

Hot Tip #6: Personal collaborations are more important than ever. For your forthcoming book, invite people who have expertise aligned with your subject to be interviewed and showcase them in your book. Benefits: In addition to adding value to your message and connections, the collaborators will have a personal interest and involvement in bringing your book forward to the public.

Hot Tip #7: If it feels daunting to write a book from start to finish, then consider participating in a collaborative book project called an "anthology." Anthologies provide an opportunity to collaborate with other thought leaders, share your insight and expertise, while you come together to reach more people as you launch and share through all of your respective reaches.

Be Generous with Introductions

When you talk with others, listen to what they are truly looking to do, build, and create. Think about the amazing and talented people you know that might be able to help them, get them on a show, support them in bringing their messages forward, and/or supporting their visions. Then facilitate the introduction. This is powerful positioning and a great visibility opportunity; it also positions you as a connector.

When I'm given an opportunity to be on a show or summit, I always ask what sort of speakers/experts they are looking for who would be supportive for their show, summit, or event. This way I'm bringing more connections to the show/summit, serving more people; and if I'm not a fit for them, then I'm still adding value and helping make these important connections.

Hot Tip #8: People want to be connected with trustworthy powerful experts who can help in meeting their needs. When you show up as someone who listens and helps people make powerful contacts, you are seen as someone who is well-connected and trustworthy.

Hot Tip #9: Don't worry about what's in it for you. Be willing to make the introduction because it serves those you are connecting. People do remember and you will be amazed at the relationships and opportunities that come to you because you were willing to lean in first.

Choose to Echo Out What Matters Most to You

Choose to be someone who stands for your truth, your people, your message, no matter what is going on around you. Let challenges give you clarity and purpose in what you are doing. Let challenges help you go deeper and fuel your purpose. The clearer you are, the more you show up rather than shrink back—especially in challenging times—the more people will see you and want to share you out. If every time people talk to you, all you talk about is how hard it is or you share something negative that happened, it brings people down. They will then be less inclined to connect and introduce you. Be mindful and purposeful in what you are sharing and how you are showing up. Use those opportunities to lift others, share what you are learning, how you are getting clarity, what you are doing to make a positive difference. This inspires others, lifts them up, and spreads you and your message further. **Be willing to be seen and shine, especially in challenging times.**

Hot Tip #10: Every day, we are more visible than we realize: when we comment on posts, share them, talk on the phone, participate in a video chat, stand in line at the grocery store. How are you showing up? What are you echoing out? Be mindful and purposeful that how you are choosing to be and what you are sharing is truly aligned with you. These are all visibility opportunities that we can choose, to share kindness, patience, love, understanding, purposefulness, peace, and hope.

Hot Tip #11: Choose to shine out what matters most to you, especially during challenging times.

The pandemic has created opportunities for us to lean in and connect. We can still build powerful relationships while bringing our messages forward, perhaps even deeper and more widespread than ever before.

Rebecca Hall Gruyter is a Global Influencer, #1 international best-selling and award-winning author, compiler, an in-demand publisher, popular radio show and podcast host (listeners on over eight networks), and an empowerment leader. She has built multiple platforms to help experts reach more people. These platforms include: radio, TV, books, magazines, the Speaker Talent Search, and live events…creating a powerful promotional reach of over ten million!

Rebecca is the CEO of RHG Media Productions, which has helped 200-plus authors become best-sellers! She has personally contributed to over thirty published books, multiple magazines, and has been quoted in major media: The Huffington Post, ABC, CBS, NBC, Fox, and Thrive Global. She has been recognized as one of the top ten working women in America by AWWIN, Inc.

Rebecca wants you to have impact! Be Seen, Heard and SHINE!

925-787-1572
www.YourPurposeDrivenPractice.com
www.RHGTVNetwork.com
www.SpeakerTalentSearch.com
Rebecca@YourPurposeDrivenPractice.com

CONNIE WHITMAN

From Unknown to Number One

Has your organization ever been ranked number one in your industry? Have you thought about being spotlighted in high-end media sites, like *Forbes* and *Money Magazine*? Is your organization the best hidden secret in your market?

Most organizations will never receive national number one recognition because they do not have a clear culture. Rather, they allow employees and division executives to do their own thing, building silos instead of collaborative, innovative cultures.

How do you build such a dynamic, productive, and inspiring culture? The answer is simple: Create a mission-driven vision that has a functioning and fluid blueprint covering the next one to five years.

Let's get your organization from being unknown to a powerhouse in your industry. Here's how…Well, some background first.

Fifteen years ago, I was hired by a commercial bank that had no culture or brand identity in their market. By 2018, it had achieved the regional rank of number one bank by *Money Magazine* and ranked in the top fifty banks, out of 8,000 nationally, by *Forbes Magazine*. Using my blueprint, it's not as hard as you may think to accomplish this level of success. It's as easy as six steps…

1. **Vision**—Vision starts at the top and works its way down. The executive team needs to be the visionaries, supporting and building a sales, service, and corporate coaching culture.

2. **Leadership**—Company visionaries should identify the project leaders who will champion the new culture and support the mission. Right out of the gate, a plan should be developed to get buy-in from the teams involved in the desired everyday culture.

3. **Communication**—Next, experts within the organization who need to be involved in the creation of the defined culture should be determined. Organization of the blueprint should be communicated to every team, division, and person involved so that they understand their roles. Create a communication platform to keep everyone in the loop, so fear can be eliminated and dynamic growth can begin.
4. **Technical Needs**—Project owners need to meet with the head of the IT department to understand the capabilities of the technical infrastructure in place. Addressing and seeking the best alternatives with software upgrades and other technical challenges is critical when building a customer-centric culture. Technology costs and implementation processes must be considered to determine what technology is needed and what costs will be incurred. Defining annual budget line items will be needed to accommodate required acquisitions and to support the long-term viability of the culture.
5. **Vendor Partnerships**—Based on discussions, external vendors may be needed for software upgrades, development, implementation of training, and other missing pieces that are or are not available within the organization's current infrastructure. Knowing when to elicit help from the outside is key. There are many unknowns when creating a fluid customer-driven culture. Outside vendors are experts and will help save time and money with proper implementation.
6. **Execution**—The leader of each division should identify employees who will remain in their current positions, the people who need to be moved to alternate positions (based on the culture being created), and estimate the percentage of people who may opt out of the changes and leave the organization through natural attrition. This is a necessary step to have the right people remain to execute the new vision and culture.

These six steps may appear oversimplified. They are not. When followed, they will lead to a dynamic culture change that moves the organization forward in becoming a powerhouse player in the market.

*****

Now, let's discuss some of the behaviors the leadership team will need to identify and address.

Fear

Part of the struggle with culture change or any organizational change is fear. People like when things remain the same and they feel comfortable. So with any change, using the above steps and implementing a clear, open channel of communication keeps everyone informed and will minimize the level of fear employees, at all levels, may experience.

Every employee needs to understand the organization's one-to-five-year strategic plan so individuals can decide whether they want to be part of the changes. It must be clear that opting out of change is not an option and that with change comes new opportunities for everyone at all levels!

Change Management

Using change-management strategies and understanding the different types of emotions that may be experienced during the change cycle are important. Build into the blueprint how naysayers who fear change and want things to stay the same will be addressed. If not addressed, the negative employees will try to sabotage every step of the implementation and may gossip behind the scenes, causing a negative undercurrent and delays—or worse: the derailment of the overall vision and execution of the plan.

By implementing change-management strategies, the organization will be able to see pitfalls along the way. Some strategies may be identifying and eliciting employees who will be included at all levels within the organization; addressing whether the changes can be accomplished using internal talent and resources only or if using an outside vendor is necessary to elevate the success of the culture changes; deciding who will manage and host the kickoff party, what will the theme and objective of the kickoff look and feel like; finally, choosing who will be the project manager, coordinating all the moving parts with the program rollout, et cetera.

Customer Service Standards

Before anything else is implemented, the executives or project owners need to define their brand identity and how the customer-facing team will support the customer's expected experience. All culture changes and expectations should have the client experience at the cornerstone of the vision.

Chick-fil-A embodies this brand identity and customer support. No matter the Chick-fil-A location, the experience is the same. Instead of saying "No problem," all employees respond by saying, "My pleasure."

"My pleasure" sounds and FEELS much more inviting and caring than "No Problem"! Anyone you ask that has been to a Chick-fil-A will say they love the customer service level of care and respect.

Setting the expectation, implementing a clear vision, getting the correct people involved from the start, and reinforcing and holding all employees accountable creates a dynamic, fluid, living culture. Why would you want anything less for your organization or business?

Outside Vendor Help

When my client was named the number one bank in their region by *Money Magazine*, it was an honor to have played a part in their achievement and to have experienced the media recognition that followed. This type of honor is not achieved overnight. Implementation, fluid design, and accountability measurements are necessary. Outside forces (pandemic), market conditions, and many other factors play a role in achieving a living and breathing culture like my client created. Defining and creating an environment of fluid change and growth within their culture was a winning combination that helped achieve the success they did.

*****

My involvement as the vendor developing the sales, service, and coaching curriculum, as well as implementing the training for all existing employees and new hires, was instrumental in building the defined culture for my client. The respectful, ongoing partnership between my client and my organization accelerated their growth from $3 billion in assets to over $10 billion during that fifteen-year period. My background as an executive in the retail division of a bank for thirteen years, and being a business consultant for twenty years, has given me the expertise to help organizations like them to create high-performing teams while generating high levels of customer engagement.

You can see what a huge, but simple, undertaking building this type of dynamic culture is and why all division heads and executive leadership teams need to commit to the changes being created. Top-down positioning is key, otherwise change will never happen. Additionally, outside help is often needed because of the number of moving parts in this type of endeavor. An expert on board who deals with developing and implementing culture change will save time and money.

Culture and branding, getting buy-in at every level, employees working together and wanting to be part of something bigger than themselves are all required for successful change. Everyone needs to know the plan—communication needs to be up, down, and all around to create this level of success.

Is your organization playing to win in your market? Are you ready to grow your business using this same blueprint/formula? Take one step at a time and see the magic happen.

Continued...

Connie Whitman is the CEO of Whitman & Associates, LLC; she is a speaker, podcast host, and author of a number one international best-seller, *ESP (Easy Sales Process)*. Her inspired teaching, transformational tools, and content ensure businesses grow income by developing profitable relationship-based connections.

Connie, as the CEO of Whitman & Associates for the past two decades, with her signature "7-Step Sales Process," has helped thousands of sales people grow and scale their businesses. She is a trusted strategic partner, building lasting relationships with innovative business owners, thought leaders, and organizations worldwide.

As a podcast host, she is thrilled to share inspiring content on her weekly, international podcasts, the *Heartfelt Sales Leader* and *Enlightenment of Change*, as a free resource for professionals looking to fast-track their careers.

https://whitmanassoc.com/
Connie@whitmanassoc.com
Free Communication Style Assessment (CSA): www.whitmanassoc.com/csa
Heart-Centered Sales Leader podcast: https://podcasts.apple.com/us/podcast/heart-centered-sales-leader/id1543243616
Enlightenment of Change Podcast: https://podcasts.apple.com/us/podcast/enlightenment-of-change/id1313299091

KELLY NAGLE

The Journey from Rock Bottom

Finding yourself at rock bottom can be a gift. Staring up at life from rock bottom and seeing bits and pieces of your existence shattered around you leaves you feeling emotionally raw. The fear, shame, and hopelessness are consuming. In that moment, you have two choices. You can remain in that state of despair and resign yourself to just moving through life trying to survive, or you can use that moment as a catalyst for tremendous transformation.

How did I find myself at rock bottom by my early thirties? There were several life events that pushed me a bit further towards rock bottom, but none as impactful as an extremely unhealthy marriage. Years of living in a toxic environment severely damaged my feelings of self-worth. My relationship fanned the flames of fear and shame until they were overpowering. I felt chronic pain from living with unfathomable levels of stress. I'd abandoned most activities I had once enjoyed since it took all my strength to manage work and marriage. I was highly anxious, always exhausted, and emotionally volatile. My self-confidence was nonexistent. I felt as if I was a passenger in a car speeding through life. I had no control, no direction. I was white-knuckling my way through each day unable to see my destination.

When my nine-year marriage ended, I realized I had been spiraling towards rock bottom for a long time. Once I was cognizant of finding myself at the bottom of a downward spiral, the climb upwards seemed daunting. I spent the next few months grappling my way through a severe traumatic reaction and tending to the deep emotional and psychological wounds that manifested from trying to make a toxic relationship work.

It took years of reflection to understand that finding myself at rock bottom wasn't as much about specific events as it was about lacking the skills to deal with them. I had ventured into adulthood ill-equipped to tackle life proactively. It wasn't my fault or anyone else's for that matter. We aren't taught about embracing self-worth or confronting fear. I didn't learn about healthy relationships or communication in school. The media isn't a model for these skills either.

Relationships are glorified for their dramatic qualities. Often, self-worth is measured by how many followers we have and whether we're subscribing to the latest trends. We've learned to define our worthiness in life by external factors. In doing so, we have willingly handed over control of our lives. We've voluntarily moved from the driver's seat in life to the passenger's side.

As I viewed life from rock bottom, I knew I had two options. I could blame my misery on my ex-husband, wallow in self-pity for a few months, then venture back onto the same path hoping for a different outcome. Or I could choose a new path. Trying the uncharted path is more difficult, but leads towards a better destination. I chose the latter and spent the next several years dedicated to self-exploration and learning how to better navigate life's challenges. I embraced therapy and confronted tough questions about my past experiences and beliefs; I explored healthier mechanisms for handling adversity and decision-making; I embarked on rediscovering my self-worth and confidence. Eventually, I built up critical skills that allowed me to, finally and permanently, be in the driver's seat.

One important realization I made was the extent to which I had allowed fear and shame to sit in the driver's seat and dictate my direction in life. As fear and shame gained more control over my emotions and decision-making, my confidence and self-worth declined. My existence was consumed by minimizing potential upheavals rather than living to be happy. As a result, I stayed in relationships even though I was miserable. I didn't leave my ex-husband sooner because I was ashamed to admit I'd married the wrong person. I feared looking like a failure for not being able to make a marriage work. I was afraid I'd never find someone else to love me. The idea of an unknown future terrified me so much that I desperately clung to the unsatisfying status quo.

Fear and shame didn't only dictate my romantic relationships; I endured unhealthy professional relationships as well. I stayed in jobs I disliked or I took jobs that didn't feel right because I feared missing an opportunity to advance. After all, status is revered by society. I also maintained platonic relationships that drained me of energy and didn't reciprocate respect. Regardless of the type of relationship, I was always at the mercy of other's needs and expectations because I was attaching my self-worth to their responses. I also feared their negative reactions because I lacked the inner strength to follow my convictions and withstand criticism.

Transforming my relationship with fear and shame was an important step in my journey back from rock bottom. Fear is a valuable emotion because it's the first warning sign that something is wrong, scary, or dangerous. Fear forces us to pause and reflect. For many years, I heard the voice of fear in my head and stopped dead in my tracks. Instead of trying new adventures, taking on big challenges, speaking up for myself, and being open to new possibilities, I retreated. At the time, I felt relief that I'd avoided something "bad." In reality, however, succumbing to fear didn't prevent negative outcomes; they happened anyway.

During my upward climb from rock bottom, I learned how to harness my fear and allow it to inform, rather than control me. Doing so has led to wonderful experiences, feeling stronger and happier than I could have imagined, and being given incredible opportunities.

What does "harnessing my fear" look like? At the end of last year, I quit my job as executive director of a highly respected non-profit organization to finish my master's degree and pursue a career I was being called to. If the situation of leaving an executive-level position for an unemployed academic one had been presented to me a few years prior, I would have said, *Heck no!* Fear of the long list of potentially catastrophic outcomes and the likely onslaught of criticism would have been too intimidating. I would have ignored my passions in favor of the status quo.

Instead of running away when fear reared its ugly head, I listened to the messages it was trying to convey. I extracted the valuable concerns about income and future employment and considered how to deal with them. Then I put in my notice. Instead of being fearful about not knowing what would come next, I felt exhilarated by all the possibilities and confident in my own abilities. I graduated with a master's degree in January 2020, ready to enter the next chapter of my life.

Then the world came to a standstill.

At that point, fear reared its ugly head once again. The demons of criticism that lived in my mind started getting louder. How would I find a job? Are people going to think I'm a failure? Should I just take any job instead of staying the course to follow my passions?

In that moment, I recognized that fear was trying to take the wheel again. Instead of recoiling or making a short-sighted decision, I used the tools I had been cultivating on my journey from rock bottom. I used the presence of fear to pause, separate the useful information from unnecessary self-criticism, and then put a game plan together that was not only feasible but also honored my personal goals. For once, I was in complete control of how I moved forward in life.

Where have my decisions taken me over the past several months? Instead of panicking about the unprecedented situation we find ourselves in or resigning myself to feeling helpless, I've viewed this year as offering unique prospects. In serendipitous fashion, amazing opportunities emerged. I've taken the leap into the very unpredictable world of entrepreneurism, both as a co-founder, working side-by-side with a trusted colleague, as well as creating my own venture to help others navigate the uncharted paths of life.

Looking back, I'm grateful for rock bottom. It was the catalyst I needed to find my courage to create a life that brings me genuine happiness.

If you find yourself at rock bottom, or on your way there, I hope you choose the uncharted path for your journey upwards.

Kelly Nagle has devoted her life to advocating for social justice and empowering others. For over a decade, Kelly worked in the nonprofit industry, leading teams, advocating for health equity, and implementing community health programs. In 2020, Kelly followed her passions for global policy and social justice by co-founding *Teen Think Tank Project*, a student-run policy institute that develops policy frameworks for real-life issues and empowers students to become future changemakers. Kelly hosts the organization's weekly podcast, *Here's the Problem*.

Kelly is also the founder of *Uncharted*, which helps clients navigate life's challenges and live the best version of themselves. *Uncharted* is dedicated to self-empowerment and guiding individuals towards finding the courage and confidence to fulfill their life's purpose.

Kelly holds a MA from Rutgers University in political science—United Nations and global policy and a BA in history from Loyola University Maryland.

Kelly lives in New Jersey with her Shetland Sheepdogs, Rachmaninoff and Penelope.

info@kellynagle.com
www.instagram.com/uncharted_community/
www.linkedin.com/company/theunchartedcommunity/
www.kellynagle.com

JULIE HOOD

Five Steps to Course Creation

"But what if I'm not an expert?" I hear this question from clients who are considering whether or not to create an online course. They are worried they aren't PhDs or don't have awards giving them permission to be a teacher. So I tell them about my first semester of college with Professor Reed.

There I was in class... a small-town girl, off in the "big city" for college, after my advisor had decided it was a good idea to put me into honors calculus as a first-semester freshman. In walks Professor Reed. He jumps to the board and starts running through complex problems. He was the top calculus expert in the department and fascinated with intricate and unique problems.

Well, I had a bigger issue... I had no calculus background. I didn't have calculus in high school. I needed someone to start from the beginning. But that wasn't what Professor Reed was interested in teaching. He didn't want to explain how to get started with calculus. He was bored with those problems!

One day, he came into class furious with us. As we sat there terrified at what was happening to our grades and seeing our scholarships fade into the distance, he started yelling at us. "I can't believe it. You guys did terrible on the last test. The regular calculus students did so much better than you did. You should be the top students getting the top grades!"

The problem was, he was too much of an expert. Sure, he knew every intricate detail of calculus and he had a PhD, but he didn't know how to help us. He couldn't relate to not knowing how to do basic problems.

The graduate students who were TAs for the regular classes knew what it was like to learn calculus from the beginning. They could explain the concepts in a way that made sense to their students.

Bottom line, you don't want to be a PhD who knows everything there is to know about your topic to teach it. You want to be ahead of your students but still be able to relate to what they need (and what they don't know).

The Five Steps to Creating an Online Course That Wows Your Students

When planning online courses, here are five steps to becoming the most popular teacher on the block.

Step 1: Find the Right Topic

Let's do an exercise. Grab a piece of paper and draw a line from the top to the bottom, then one from left to right so you have four boxes on the sheet—four places to record your research for your course.

1. **Search for Facebook groups in your topic area.** Look at what questions are asked frequently or have lots of comments. These are the topics people feel most "pained" around and the ones they are most interested in finding a solution to (and potentially paying for!). In the top left box of your paper, write "Facebook Groups" and record your findings. I did this with a Facebook group for course creators. A question asked often was, "Where should I host a course?" So I created a free mini-course where I answer that exact question (sign up at www.CourseCreatorsHQ.com/ee).

2. **Then visit Amazon.** Write "Amazon books" in the top right box of your piece of paper. Look for books available in your topic area; read their table of contents to see the topics. I did this and found a book about online courses. One of the chapter titles was "How to Validate Your Course Idea." So I created a free mini-course on this topic too. It's called, "Is My Idea Any Good?" (You can get it at www.CourseCreatorsHQ.com/ee).

3. **Next, check out course marketplaces.** Course marketplaces are websites that sell courses. You can use them to gauge the interest in a topic (but please don't look at their pricing). These sites tend to undercharge and underpay the creators. I want you to get an idea of what topics are out there and are already being sold. Check out Udemy.com, Skillshare.com, and LinkedInLearning.com. Review the course modules and see what topics are covered. Are they ones you could teach? For example, I found a

course on Udemy about creating courses. It talked about validating your idea, so I knew that was a great topic for my mini-course.

Remember though, if you use these sites, you may not control the pricing or how much you are paid per course. I want you to have a course you can charge hundreds of dollars for—or a lot more—per student. Use the sites for research and make notes in the bottom left box.

4. **Finally, search YouTube.** YouTube is the second most popular search engine in the world after Google; find some videos about your topic for your fourth box. Enter different phrases for your topic—general, high-level phrases, and more specific, detailed phrases.

   Review the comments on the videos to help identify what people don't know. By including concepts perceived to be missing or "not covered," you will add value to your course.

After spending a few hours on this research, you should have an excellent idea about what topics are the most important to your target audience. You'll know what they don't know—and where they are looking for more answers.

From your research, pick a very specific topic of "transformation" or "change" that you can teach—but it won't include everything you know about the topic. Make sure it fills in the blank: "How to _____."

Step 2: Outline the Course—In No Time Flat!

Next, come up with an outline for your course by creating a framework around the solution. For example, I created a course framework that breaks into twenty-four hours—one hour at a time. Students work through the steps, hour-by-hour: some folks spend a three-day weekend and crank out their course in three eight-hour days; others spend one hour a day for twenty-four days. This framework makes my course unique—and it helps with sales.

One of the biggest mistakes I see course creators making is trying to put everything they know into one course. This is a big mistake! Offer just enough that your students can get to the finish line.

Here are two ways to outline your course. Pick the one that feels the easiest for you.

- **#1: Create a list of topics that could be included. Put them in a logical order.** What does your student need to know first? second? third? What topics could be left out? What topics could be added? Ideally, include four to six main "modules" with four to six "lessons" for each module. If you have more than this, consider creating a second course.

Or…

- **#2: Grab a stack of index cards or Post-it notes and list one topic on each card.** Then sort and arrange them into a logical order with modules and lessons.

Step 3: Create Course Content

Next, create a cheat sheet, similar to *Cliff Notes*, to summarize each lesson. Then hop on your phone or computer and create an audio for each lesson. You can create a video too if you like—but videos are not required! Your course can contain the cheat sheets and the audios to get started. You can always expand it later.

Step 4: Host Your Course

In Step 4, find an online platform to put the cheat sheets and audios you have created so you can share them with your students. There are some fantastic tools online for hosting courses—sites like Kajabi, Teachable, and Thinkific are three I especially like.

Step 5: Set Up Your Sales Page

Finally, you need a way to sell your course. Most of the hosting tools will provide a sales page where, with a click of a button, people can buy your course. On the sales page, include:

- A headline that pulls in potential students
- A discussion of the problem you solve and the transformation you are promising
- The steps involved in your framework
- A testimonial or two from people you have worked with in the past
- "Buy" buttons spread throughout the page and at the very bottom

*****

There you have it! Five simple steps to creating your first course. Please let me know if you use this process and tell me all about your new course. I can't wait to hear about your success!

Julie Hood: Five Steps to Course Creation

Julie Hood of CourseCreatorsHQ.com helps authors, experts, coaches, and consultants create and market amazing online courses. She believes that courses and training can change and improve the world when experts share their knowledge. Julie has been online since the dark ages of the Internet when she started selling an ebook. She now helps her students and clients go from idea to finished course to selling six and seven figures online.

Interested in knowing more? Be sure to check out her free mini-trainings at https://www.CourseCreatorsHQ.com/ee.

And if you decide to create an online course, contact Julie before signing up for your course hosting. She offers some incredible bonuses when people sign up for Kajabi, Teachable and Thinkific.

Connect with Julie:
www.CourseCreatorsHQ.com/podcast
www.Facebook.com/CourseCreatorsHQ
www.Instagram.com/CourseCreatorsHQ
www.CourseCreatorsHQ.com/YouTube
www.Twitter.com/CourseCreatorsHQ

DR. MAURYA D. COCKRELL

The SDoH Solutionary

I am pretty skeptical about the work-life balance concept. We are told to believe we must achieve a perfect balance between our professional and personal lives. Is it possible for each area of our lives to operate in a silo? My answer is no.

I believe that we are interconnected, interdependent, and interrelated beings. As an INFJ (Introvert, Intuitive, Feeling, Judging personality type), I have one of the world's rare personality traits. My ability to serve as a dreamer and doer allows me to identify problems and solutions uniquely. I am a profoundly relational being that sees the connection between people and the world around them.

In this complex, entangled system of life, we encounter challenges daily. Issues of healthcare, job security, economic stability, housing, and social community are on our minds 24/7.

I found my calling as "The Solutionary" because I am more than a problem-solver. I see unsuitable and unsustainable interconnected problems and use compassion and stewardship to design strategic, interdisciplinary solutions. Our lives impact the organizations we work for, which affects our communities, and impacts our society. As a coach and consultant, I have learned that the interplay between living, working, and learning determines my clients' quality of life.

Since we are interdependent beings, it is essential to understand the concept of advocacy. Advocacy is the act of supporting oneself, others, or social change. Life will always come with challenges and setbacks, but it is essential to understand our needs and be a champion for ourselves. We need self-advocacy strategies in the workplace, in our communities, and when it comes to our education and healthcare. For example, we need to advocate for stretch assignments, promotions, and raises in the workplace. Being able to negotiate and explain our valuable contribution to the company is self-advocacy in action.

In addition to looking out for our own best interests, we must include group advocacy. Remember, we are interconnected beings. Therefore, to have a successful organization, we should advocate for others when the opportunity arises. We should find joy in serving and fighting for the best treatment for others. Can you imagine the beautiful culture and climate we could create if we could only look past ourselves?

Next, we can work on systems advocacy. This is how we change the world! Imagine living in a society where we review laws, policies, and procedures to ensure every individual feels valued, included, and empowered.

There is a strong relationship between advocacy and stewardship. Stewardship is the responsibility for managing the resources we are given. It is advocacy in action that holds us accountable for the change we uphold in our lives, our organizations, and our communities. Stewardship also makes us responsible for one another. I am a firm believer that we should care for others and always leave the world a better place than how we entered it.

Takeaways:

- You are your own best champion. Advocate for the life you have dreamed of and then pay it forward.
- Stewardship is grounded in responsibility and accountability. In our interrelated world, we must take care of the resources we have (i.e., health, economic, environmental, social, and educational).

As a coach, I guide my clients on a pathway to solutions with an interrelated approach. For example, I have worked with a client who struggled with job satisfaction and fulfillment. Through coaching, we addressed what an ideal career environment would look like; and with that vision, we worked backward on a pathway to achieve her goals.

The solution was not as simple as applying for an internal opening or leaving the company. Instead, we continued to analyze her strengths and weaknesses so she could ask her management for job enlargement. You see, the answer was not a vertical transition but a horizontal one that allowed her exposure to new tasks that reduced boredom. Keeping in mind the interplay of vocation and health, the solution allowed her to decrease burnout and absenteeism in the workplace.

When looking at organizational health, many companies struggle to find solutions to toxic cultures and climates. Organizational culture is the employees' shared set of values and beliefs, but the climate is how they experience the environment. It is the overall tone. While we spend countless hours and dollars focused on inclusion initiatives, we fail to focus on the actual results and changed behavior that stems from those initiatives.

Executive leaders often contact my organization to conduct diversity training. When they do, I like to introduce my "Give, Lead, Open Opportunities, and Work" (GLOW) framework for corporate social responsibility. GLOW training is a comprehensive approach to diversity, equity, and inclusion (DEI). A comprehensive approach to DEI assesses how organizations give back to the community, become industry leaders for inclusiveness, provide opportunities for advancement to minorities, and create volunteer opportunities sponsored by the workplace. Viewing the workplace climate and community as interrelated sets my DEI programming apart from other organizations. With the GLOW framework, organizational leaders learn how to glean insight into what their employees value and how to connect to their lives outside of work.

Again, we are complex and interdependent beings. Social justice issues stem from stereotypes and biases developed from our upbringing and society. We cannot have the audacity to think employees perform efficiently and effectively when civil unrest is outside their front doors. Without allowing an employee to bring their whole self to work, how can the culture and climate genuinely change?

Takeaways:

- Grab the steering wheel of your life. Use coaching as a mechanism to reach your professional and personal goals.
- Do not settle on a job; instead, find a vocation. Tap into an organization where you can bring your whole being to work. And if you find yourself in a situation of misalignment, advocate for organizational equity and encourage leaders to have honest conversations about the culture and climate.

- Follow the GLOW Framework:
  - Give
  - Lead
  - Open Opportunities
  - Work
* Understand the importance of community. If you see someone in social isolation or lacking a supportive network, extend an invitation and be inclusive.

A solutionary goes beyond the role of a problem-solver. Solutionaries are not fueled by curiosity but, instead, motivated by compassion and purpose. To us, situations, good and bad, are interconnected and require complex strategic solutions.

In 2015, I founded YKNOT Consulting, a boutique stewardship solutions firm. At YKNOT, our solutions are comprehensive and interdisciplinary. We value the importance of working across various fields of expertise to re-envision problems and solutions.

To every solution, we apply the same framework:

First, it is crucial to **yield** (produce). As advocates and stewards, we should always be in the mindset of producing good for ourselves, organizations, and society.

Second, it is necessary to gain **knowledge**. Not only is it important to value traditional and non-traditional education, but it is also vital to gain an understanding of the challenges we are facing. For example, organizations cannot build a change management strategy without knowing the current work climate and the reason behind the need for change.

Third, it is key to develop strong **networks**. As we discussed, as interconnected beings, we should have social, professional, and spiritual networks. We cannot reach our fullest potential if we are siloed.

Fourth, it is important to review our **outlooks** to produce meaningful outcomes. As we often see in diversity and inclusion work, we cannot produce significant outcomes if we cannot change individuals' outlooks. People must first become aware of their biases to learn how to reduce and eliminate them.

Last, it is important to develop **talent**. No matter what stage we are in life, we should strive to find the talent within ourselves and others. If we cannot see our value and self-worth, it will be harder for others to see it. That said, being realistic, we all have moments of self-doubt. We are all designed with a specific and unique skill set, and we are destined to complete a pathway that no one else can. And if ever you need a little help finding that pathway, call me, The Solutionary.

Takeaways:

When you notice someone is struggling with feeling valued, heard, and accepted, be the one to encourage them to use their gifts.

When life throws obstacles your way, remember the values of advocacy and stewardship.

Remember the YKNOT Framework
- Yield
- Knowledge
- Networks
- Outlooks/outcomes
- Talent

Best wishes on your YKNOT and GLOW journey. – Dr. Maurya.

Continued…

Dr. Maurya D. Cockrell is an established SDoH Solutionary from St. Louis, Missouri. She holds a BS in health management from Saint Louis University, with a minor in theological studies, an MA from Webster University in human resources management, and a doctorate in health professions education from Logan University. She has received additional training and certifications, including Senior Professional in Human Resources (SPHR), SHRM Senior Certified Professional (SHRM-SCP), Evidence-Based Design (EDAC), Legal and Ethical Issues in Healthcare, Social Entrepreneurship, Executive Coaching, Career Coaching, and Human Resources Consulting. Dr. Cockrell uses serial entrepreneurship, education, and community collaboration to improve how people live, learn, work, and play.

Dr. Cockrell founded YKNOT Consulting in 2015. YKNOT Consulting is a boutique stewardship solutions firm specializing in consulting and coaching. Grounded in a stewardship philosophy, YKNOT offers comprehensive interdisciplinary solutions to economic, educational, social, wellness, and community challenges.

Dr. Cockrell is a proud member of Delta Sigma Theta Sorority, Inc.

Dr. Maurya Dominica Cockrell
314-304-2051
info@consultyknot.com
ConsultYKNOT.com
linktr.ee/drmauryadominica

CINDY ROWAN

Leadership Development: From Myths to Impact

Now more than ever, we hear about the urgency for great leaders in organizations. It's not surprising that leadership development is such a hot topic today; and quite frankly, it should be at the top of the list! Think about it. Every business has competition that offers somewhat similar products/services; and while businesses like to boast about their unparalleled customer service, what about the leadership qualities of people who represent those products and services to customers? Having specific job expertise is important, but what about such leadership qualities as empathy, resilience, influence, positivity, integrity, and personal accountability, to name a few? Might these not be the true differentiating factors that can make an organization standout from its competition?

During my twenty-five-plus years of experience as a consulting partner to a variety of organizations, I've seen the plethora of benefits that organizations (and their employees) have realized by developing leaders at all levels; however, it's interesting to note how they progress in that journey.

Typically, a client will engage my services because a particular pressure point is driving their perceived need to develop leaders. Sometimes the pressure is the need to create the next generation of leaders or to enhance such attributes with folks who weren't developed along the way. Occasionally, I sense their reasoning to develop leaders is because it's "the thing to do." Identifying the pressure is important; and from there, it's wise to address some common myths about leadership development and focus on strategies aimed toward developing leaders at all levels.

Let's first take a look at some of those myths and then explore a model that can help make a difference.

Myth 1: The Terms "Leadership" and "Management" Are Interchangeable.

No. Leadership and management are not the same! Look around. Folks may have great management skills, but lack the ability to influence and align others. Similarly, some leaders can create a vision but may not be adept at managing time and resources to execute that vision. Clearly, defining what "leadership" and "management" are in an organization is critical. If you find no difference between the two, something's wrong!

Myth 2: Leadership Development Is Geared Toward a Certain Level of Employees Within an Organization.

False. A common misnomer in organizations is that leadership development is reserved for the most senior folks or any employee who has direct reports. This false belief perpetuates Myth 1.

Defining leadership by title only is limiting. Effective leadership development taps into the real potential of every employee. Many shakers and movers within business ranks can engage others, and even influence change and champion innovation. That's leadership! Leveraging these qualities contributes not only to individual growth but also undergirds a healthy organizational culture.

Many times when discussing leadership development with clients, the subject turns to succession planning. Typically, organizations communicate that a well-developed process has been undertaken to identify heir-apparents. However, often, there is not much substance to individual development planning and action. Again, this seems to be limited to a select group when all employees need to continuously develop.

Myth 3: Leadership Development Is a Training Program.

No, no, and no! Maybe training is a tool to foster leadership development, but it is not a stand-alone event. Too often, organizations take only a programmatic approach to leadership development. Often, the impact and sustainability of these well-intentioned *programs* leave something to be desired. Many times, these programs address management skills, not leadership qualities, and there may be no follow up.

Effective leadership development is an integral part of an organization's culture. It supports the notion, *We want every employee to be a leader. This is what it means in our organization; it is an expectation. We invest in people because they are valuable assets and impact our success.* Leadership development is strategic in every sense.

For this development to be impactful, it needs to be a holistic approach that taps into a person's values, influences, and behaviors; not just a random set of skills. Then within the context of what's needed/expected by the organization, plans for how one can use leadership to grow as a person and maximize their contribution to the organization need to connect. Training, along with support initiatives like coaching and mentoring, need to be designed as a part of an on-going journey throughout one's career and life!

Myth 4: Leadership Comes with Experience.

False. Experience does not equal ability! Longevity doesn't make employees relevant and capable leaders. Technical expertise is commendable, but it's not leadership. Leadership development is dynamic, not static. That said, it's obvious that experience and leadership don't go hand-in-hand. Leadership needs to be cultivated through self-assessment, feedback, coaching, and thoughtful development planning. Experience adds frame of reference to the leadership development process. Through experiences, we learn more about ourselves, how we can apply our leadership attributes and grow through role models who can offer good and not-so-good examples to emulate (or not).

Myth 5: Leadership Development Is an Expense.

Wrong. I shudder when I hear the term "expense" related to any kind of development, particularly leadership development! Leadership development is an investment. It is an expense when its value is not realized or there is no actual return on investment or expectation to follow through. Organizations need to determine the importance and positive impact developing leaders at all levels can have.

*****

Identifying the myths and addressing the barriers to fruitful leadership development is a great start. But then what?

Consider a five-step model of leadership development for your organization that will have high impact.

1. Define, Assess, and Determine Measurable Outcomes

Assess what's driving the need for leadership development in your organization. Seek different perspectives in the process. Define how leadership development ties into your strategic vision and corporate culture. What leadership skills and behaviors are needed and expected? Why?

Determining outcomes should focus on two levels: (1) how effective leadership will impact your business and (2) how it will impact individuals. How will you measure this on both levels?

2. Champion Leadership Development from the Highest Level in the Organization

Leadership development is as important as any other business initiative impacting profitability. It needs to be embraced in the C-Suite and clearly understood throughout the organization. Studies suggest that without support at all levels any type of leadership strategy has less than a fifty percent chance of being impactful. Overcommunicate about what your organization's philosophy and expectations are for leaders. How does it fit within your culture? Keep leadership development at the forefront of business and team discussions, as well as individual performance criteria.

3. Create a Model and Test It

After analyzing the information in Step 1, consider how a leadership development model will take form. At this juncture, training and development support pieces can be considered within the overall context of leadership development. Contemplate a variety of options that fit the needs of your desired culture. Experiential learning bolsters any type of training while providing employees an opportunity to practically apply and assess their leadership learnings. Such experiences could include meaningful projects, special assignments, cross-functional team endeavors, et cetera. Foster dynamic and sustainable leadership development through an infrastructure that embodies ongoing coaching, assessment, and feedback that makes a difference.

4. Implement

The emphasis on leadership development needs to focus on its impact to the organization and employees. As previously stated, without intentional communication and envisioned expectations from the top that every employee is a leader, leadership development will be viewed as only training or a passing fad. Leadership development drives competitive advantage of the organization and, in turn, is designed to show the value of and investment in every employee. It all needs to tie together in implementation and reinforcement.

5. Evaluate, Sustain, and Celebrate!

Leadership development effectiveness should be evaluated as rigorously as any other business initiative. (i.e., How is leadership development impacting the business, the customer, the individual?). Challenge development practices that may have been around for a while. Are they relevant and impactful or are you just saying "We do it"? Celebrate the best practices of leadership in action within your organization. Showcase the individuals who are growing in their leadership journey and making a difference.

How might you take action to develop leaders at all levels?

Dispel the myths and commit to continuously reviewing the above five steps to maximize impact. Imagine the benefits to both your organization and your employees!

Continued…

Dr. Cindy Rowan serves as president of Performance Management Solutions, a consulting firm she established in 1992. Her firm helps organizations improve profitability through organizational and talent development. Dr. Rowan's expertise in designing and implementing initiatives in the areas of leadership and management excellence, creation of coaching cultures, and performance management has yielded significant growth to the clients that she serves.

As an adjunct professor, Dr. Rowan instructs graduate level courses in human resource training and development, as well as organizational behavior and development. Her specialized firm, Performance Management Solutions for Higher Education, is dedicated to assisting colleges and universities in developing cultures of service excellence and leaders at all levels.

Dr. Rowan has received numerous honors for her work and has made presentations at local, national, and international conferences on topics related to training, leadership development, and mentoring. Her doctoral degree is from Seton Hall University in New Jersey.

Cindy@perfms.com
perfms@aol.com
perfms.com
www.linkedin.com/in/cynthia-rowan-44a15712/
www.facebook.com/Performance-Management-Solutions-102326731579668/?ref=page_internal
twitter.com/PerfmsRowan

DEB GAUT

Big, Bold, Audacious Change

I wish I could tell you what happened that fateful day. Unfortunately, my mind persists in protecting me…so there's still only darkness. Colleagues later shared bits and pieces. A worrying walk to lunch. A food tray left untouched. A sudden disappearance. A glimpse of a woman circling the parade ground. An ambulance ride to the hospital—all perplexing events.

What I recall *before* that day is the arrival of a new senior executive who slowly and painstakingly dismantled everything we had built. And a protracted war of words over a direct order I had been given requiring unethical behavior on my part. (I refused to play.) Month upon month, he was sadistic and abusive. He seemed to relish in bringing us to our knees—so much so that all I could tell the doctors that day was, "My boss broke my head. My boss broke my head. My boss broke my head," whispered over and over like some sacred mantra. Laugh-out-loud sad, but true.

What I remember *after* returning to work is little more than a blur. I was experiencing lasting effects of *transient global amnesia*—my body's way of coping with extreme mental and emotional anguish. I cannot remember how long I stayed in that job: weeks? months? longer? Ultimately, I was able to secure another position for a few more months, but by then I was well and truly broken. Survival instinct kicked in. I summoned the courage to walk away from a six-figure income, an organization that I loved, and a mission to which I had sworn an oath. I knew I would never work for anyone again except myself and would devote the rest of my life to helping others through challenging transitions.

> *"Yeah, that happened. Now, move on."* – Mary Englebreit, Artist

With forty-plus years of experience working in the business, government, and academic worlds—and more than a few challenging personal and professional transitions—I have learned three universal truths about big, bold, audacious change. To survive and thrive, you must learn to:

- Master your mindset
- Energize the process
- Hold fast to your dreams

In fact, I so believe in the power of these truths that I spent eighteen months pursuing not one but three professional coaching certifications to help others accomplish these feats, then twelve months capturing them in a book called *Morph, Pivot, Launch: Navigating Your Job Search in Turbulent Times*. Following is a quick, crash course designed to introduce you to these three concepts.

Master Your Mindset

Mastering your mindset requires deep inner work—and learning to trust and believe in YOU. A good place to begin is by answering the question, *Who is the person I need to become to navigate this crisis and move boldly toward my dreams?* The bigger and bolder your dreams, the more courageous, committed, and determined you must be to becoming that person.

Resolving to become a "marathoner" is a perfect example. If you dream of running 26.2 miles and have only run short distances, you will need to become *someone who thinks, plans, trains, and acts like a marathoner*: fiercely committed; fanatical about building strength and endurance; keenly aware of the mental fortitude required to conquer long runs (and treat rest days as actual training days); and inordinately patient, knowing it takes time to build a proper foundation. For a runner, that means a year of running three to four times per week to create a solid base before launching into a marathon training program.

Take a moment and think about the person you need to become to follow your dreams. What thoughts do you need to think? What plans do you need to develop? What actions do you need to take to make your vision a reality?

Energize the Process

Being successful in any worthy endeavor requires knowing that our energy and engagement are a direct function of our thoughts, because *our thoughts drive our feelings and our feelings drive our actions.* Think about the incredible power of this simple statement. If you *think* you can do something awesome, then you will do everything in your power to actualize that goal or objective. If you think you cannot, then you "can't" and "won't" because you will devote little or no energy to making it happen. The more powerful and focused your thoughts, the more committed and enthusiastic you will be about a task at hand. The more excited you become about what you are doing, the more engaged you will be with the process. In short, as energy increases, engagement increases. The two are inextricably bound. Crazy, right? Remember how the process works: thoughts → feelings → actions.

Hold Fast to Your Dreams

When considering a major job, career, or life transition, we often begin with a singular goal in mind (e.g., escaping a terrible boss, finding more satisfying work, leaving a volatile relationship). Such a longing for change is completely understandable. However, in the process, we can easily limit our thinking to the immediate situation without considering our hopes and dreams for the future. The difference is enormous—like playing checkers instead of chess. Using "big-picture, blue-sky thinking," we can widen the aperture and plan short-term and long-term steps more strategically.

Big-picture, blue-sky thinking essentially involves three tasks: (1) creating a "bucket list" of *wishes* (i.e., meaningful, exciting, rewarding things you want to do, experience, and accomplish); (2) developing a three-year *vision* that includes the high-level steps you will take to accomplish that vision; and (3) identifying the *memories* you want to make in the process. The latter will give you a sense of equilibrium and help you focus on a more "in the moment" approach to creating your immediate future.

Why include your bucket list of wishes in the mix? Because if you start with a well-defined list, you can easily identify the steps to get the ball rolling and create a plan to make your wishes come true sooner. For example, if you have always wanted to be a foster parent for a dog or cat, why not learn about the process now?

A quick Google search nets the following six steps recommended by Petfinder.com: "(1) Find shelters and rescue groups near you; (2) Contact the organization about their foster needs and for a foster application; (3) Evaluate applications carefully (and ask good questions - e.g., Who is responsible for paying vet and food bills?); (4) Complete application process; (5) Bring home your foster dog (or cat); and (6) Smile and cry at the same time when he (or she) finds his (or her) forever home."

Experiencing forward movement with a single wish can fire up your energy and engagement in other areas of your life and transition (i.e., a job search or career change). Start dreaming and start doing. Taking little steps count.

Similarly, crafting a clear three-year vision statement can make all the difference according to world-class executive coach, Rich Litvin. If you long to make a living while traveling the world, then write it down. If you yearn to make a difference for children in war-torn nations, then write it down. Let that dream serve as the foundation of your three-year vision, then work backwards in time from there. What would you need to be doing two years from now, one year from now, six months from now, three months from now, and one month from now to make your vision a reality? Write it down. This exercise isn't for the faint of heart. It's for dreamers and doers who are passionate about taking control of their destinies.

Finally, consider memories you want to create in the coming year. With no guarantees for the future, planning memories you want to make NOW for yourself (and with your family, friends, and loved ones) will keep you grounded and excited—whether that's skydiving, hiking the Appalachian Trail, or tucking your children into bed every night. Taking time to articulate your desired memories can help you stay present in the moment, especially when you're going through difficult times.

Mastering your mindset, energizing the process, and holding fast to your dreams are the truths I have discovered in my own life. If you want or need help with a big transition, reach out to a career | transition coach. We can help.

Deb Gaut: Big, Bold, Audacious Change

As a transformation and performance coach, Deb Gaut brings a passion and vitality to helping others reconnect with their dreams and energize their careers. Her personal journey tells the story of bold moves and successful transitions—from academia to business, government, and entrepreneurship.

After 9/11 and thirty-plus years as a university professor, trainer, and consultant, Deb joined the US Department of Defense for seven years. Throughout her career, she has enjoyed teaching and mentoring others in strategies, knowledge, and skills to effectively pursue their careers. "I'm devoted to helping people leverage the remarkable power of visualization, mindset, and core energy to do what they really love," says Deb.

Today, in addition to her thriving coaching practice, she is a speaker, writer, and founding editor of *Boomalally Magazine*. Deb holds a PhD in communication and three professional coaching certifications. Her most recent book is titled *Morph, Pivot, Launch: Navigate Your Job Search in Turbulent Times*.

deb@boomalally.com
debgaut.life
MorphPivotLaunch.com
boomalally.com
linkedin.com/in/deborah-gaut/

TRISH HALL

Art of Living Spiritually

The art of living spiritually is the integration of one's whole self. When mastered, there is no spiritual life and human life, no divine life and egoic life. When living spiritually, there is a moment-by-moment recognition of Oneness—of Spirit in and as all that is. There is no separation or compartmentalism. Life is whole, inseparable from the Creator and all aspects of creation. Such a life is characterized by resilience, nonresistance, ease, grace, and peace of mind.

Often, I encounter people who have spirituality tangled with religion and yet are able to distinguish their sense of spirit apart from their religious practice. Spirituality is sensed as something greater than being human—that is not limited by one's humanity and is sometimes associated with life energy rather than physicality.

I believe that this is true of all beings. We share a common divine essence. Some recognize their own divinity—some acknowledge the divinity of all creation. Some deny this as hogwash. Others sense it, yet can't identify it: they struggle and stress trying to reconcile what they intuit with their materialistic, mechanistic understanding of the world of form.

Here is where I come in. I am a spiritual teacher, an empath and a coach ready to guide and companion journeyers as they assimilate the art of living spiritually.

I support people in responding to that nudge from within to reveal and express their pent-up uniqueness. Imagine the grand tapestry our world would be if everyone joyously shared their best, most expressive talents for the benefit of all. Wouldn't that be glorious!

Shortly before her passing at age ninety, my mother told me, "You always were a strange child—now you're grown and still strange." I laughed, accepting a truth I had always sensed. I realized that my parents' insistence that I conform to societal norms was more about not causing them embarrassment than their concern for my comfort. They didn't know how to deal with a daughter who could sense things others didn't. I learned that I needed to hide my real self in order to be acceptable.

Have you ever gotten the message that expressing yourself genuinely was not okay? That your authenticity was flawed?

Our authenticity cannot be less than precious. It is the unique expression of Spirit. To be truly authentic is extraordinary. It requires removal of masks, release of assumed identities—perhaps to be a nonconformist or a conformist by choice, not conditioning. Authentically expressing your uniqueness is the sharing of our Creator's gifts. Embrace it! Embrace you!

You possess a unique array of spiritually imbued gifts and talents. You are Spirit's dissemination system. If you withhold or deny your gifts, you are depriving yourself and the world of those particular gifts of Spirit. Have you ever looked back and thought "If only…"? Does the thought of others knowing your hidden treasures please or scare you? Some who are well acquainted with their gifts, yet never encountered anyone who recognized how truly amazing they were, utter huge sighs of relief that someone finally saw and heard them.

Shining a light on people's unexpressed abilities (what I recognize in them rather than what they believe about themselves) and challenging them to fulfill their magnificence can produce short-run chaos yet yield huge long-term benefits. If the attributes that are evident to me collide with the person's self-concept (and who doesn't have at least a smattering of self-doubt), the results can be tumultuous as with one of my students who internalized my insights as "unrealistic expectations." She so radiated innate abilities that I feared the challenge I was placing before her might be insultingly low. My perception and hers were so different that, amid a gale of tears, she railed at me about how cruel I was to impose such horribly high expectations.

Have you ever so completely identified with the roles you play in other people's worlds that you have detached from your own truth? For a time, I did. I so completely intermingled my identity with my roles that I lost touch with "my truth." The more perfectly I performed my roles, the emptier and emptier

I became. When my authenticity was challenged, I protested vociferously that I wasn't a phony—I wasn't pretending—I was the best, fullest, most genuine me I could be. Now, I work with people to remove their assumed identities and unveil authentic possibilities.

If, by chance, you are one of the many people who have blinded themselves, at least partially, to their magnificence, I invite you to embrace your full potential—to recognize your divinely imbued abilities.

You may be tempted to stop reading because of the contrast between your present self-concept and what you suspect might be wanting to be expressed. I challenge you to not run away. Release your fear-induced resistance—lean into the discomfort, kindle your curiosity, and awaken to possibility-thinking.

A client who took that challenge had been performing her roles so expertly she was dying inside. She, like many, "had put others first." She was convinced that if she were to really be real, it would take something (time, energy, resources) from those others in her life. Quite the contrary! When we withhold, we teach withholding. When we diminish or deprecate, we teach self-diminishment and self-deprecation. These are not the messages we want to impart. Living spiritually, she grasped how not stifling herself called forth the brilliance of others. The ripples of authenticity fanned out around her. She realized that sharing uniqueness has more to do with selflessness than selfishness. Having learned this lesson myself, I get to draw back the drapes and fling open the doors so others' genius and radiance may shine.

Sudden awareness of latent gifts and talents may cause discomfort and disorientation. Whether you repressed them to be acceptable or avoid criticism is irrelevant. The sadness of regret keeps you stuck in the past. In this moment, the choices you make cast how the rest of your life unfolds. It is never too late to share your gifts.

There is an art to living spiritually in a world that often does not feel spiritual. Some people make spirituality seem complicated. I come from a different perspective. I believe living spiritually is totally natural and incredibly simple: Remember what you are and express your divine uniqueness to the utmost. What you are is a spiritual being engaged in life as a human. Does your life reflect what you are—the spiritual truth of you? How recently have you reviewed your beliefs about yourself and your world, and taken inventory of your gifts, talents, abilities, and aptitudes? If you are like most people, you are overdue. Stop what you are doing and take care of it now.

Look realistically at how you are expressing your unique treasures. Consider where and when they are bringing you joy. Now is a perfect time to shed whatever may be between you and that rich sense of fulfillment when we feel "on purpose."

Many people strive for years to find their purpose, looking outside themselves when the answer has always been at hand, waiting to be acknowledged. Draw on resources. Reconnect with the divine thread that has always been present in you. The answers revealed in your inventory are the essential elements of your purpose—the keys to living spiritually at all times in constant remembrance that it's all Spirit.

As with the fulfillment of all worthwhile endeavors, mastering the art of living spiritually involves processes, practices, and commitment. It begins with acceptance of your whole self, including recognition that your current habits are reinforcing behaviors that are ripe for change. There are no quick fixes—embodying shifts and creating new neuro-pathways requires dedication.

Developing the art of living spiritually involves three steps:

1. Awakening to the truth of your authentic magnificence
2. Revealing and activating your unique attributes—putting them into full expression
3. Embracing the courage, confidence, and joy of life (your natural tools and strategies) to live vibrantly

The art of living spiritually cannot be compartmentalized. As you lean into expressing your authentic self in one area, that genuineness will leak into others. You get to choose where to focus initially; however, gradually, your entire life will be transformed, uplifting, energizing, and de-stressing all your experiences.

Lean into living your spirituality. Be your radiant, authentic self—your "best yet to be"!

Therisia "Trish" Hall, M.Div., is truly a renaissance woman. A voracious, lifelong learner, she combines her curiosity with inquiry and listening to glean in-depth understanding of her many experiences. Those experiences range from local and worldwide studies to conversations with great scholars and engagement with students and individual clients.

An insightful international best-selling author and speaker, Trish blends wisdom, authenticity, humor, and compassion. Whether addressing an audience, facilitating communication among diverse populations, working with students or individual clients, she thrives on awakening the unique magnificence within each, empowering them to live their "best yet to be."

The visionary spiritual leader of Center for Spiritual Living Metro (Greater Washington DC Metro area) and founder of Way2Peace, which promotes honoring the dignity of all life, Trish is active with Fairfax County Clergy Council, Interfaith Council of Washington, DC, Tysons Interfaith, and the Parliament of World Religions.

trishhall.unltd@gmail.com
www.trishhallunltd.com
www.cslmetro.org
www.way2peace.org
www.facebook.com/Trish-Hall-Unltd-105460331127435
www.linkedin.com/in/trish-hall-3898016/

DR. GLENN T. MILLER

Ace of All Trades

"What do you want to be when you grow up?" We all had to answer this question so many times as children; and even more so, we ask ourselves, "What do I want to do for the rest of my life?" Almost eighty percent of students in the United States change their major at least once in college; only twenty-seven percent of those who graduate college work in their field-related major! I'm sure you know one or two people, possibly yourself, that have dealt with a similar problem. You have an entire degree, declared your specialty, and yet your earnings are from something completely different. That is frustrating, especially since we are made to believe that if we don't specialize in our declared major, we must be a failure. No one wants to be the "Jack of all trades and master of none."

Now, before we dive into this oxymoronic lifestyle, let us define who exactly we are discussing. A "neo-prenuer" (as defined by myself) is an individual who is actively looking to optimize their lifestyle by creating enough capital stability to gain financial freedom. We can recognize these individuals by their characteristics: They are innately ambitious, compassionate, inquisitive, persevering, self-motivated, and determined. Neo-prenuers are top-tier problem-solvers; they are goal-oriented, and you would be very surprised at the solutions they are capable of providing. Are you a neo-prenuer?

If you are but are not living it, there is one thing that holds you back the most: the fear of being "master of none." The neo-prenuer is often known for excelling in one great skill. One of my favorite comedic actors, Adam Sandler, star of movies, *Water Boy*, *Big Daddy*, and *Wedding Singer*, has been forever typecast as the immature "man-child," which is why fans were shocked to see his latest American thriller, *Uncut Gems*, where he plays a more serious entrepreneur.

When we think of someone, it is human nature to think of them under a specific category. Whether it's our mom, our co-worker, a life-long friend, or boss, it's all too easy to typecast them into one category. But why? It's a defensive mechanism that helps us to avoid cognitive dissonance, or mental discomfort, whenever we think of that person. To put it plainly, we don't like to work too hard to identify someone. So, a dentist is just a dentist; a sales clerk is just a salesclerk; and a man-child is just a man-child. So how do people see you?

No one person is meant to be just one thing. We all wear different hats. A father, who was once a student, is now a business consultant, a professor, an entrepreneur, a motivational speaker, an author, an investor, and a doctor. Yet we are wired to filter through all of the assortment of information to simplify and identify right away. This is known as the "primacy effect" or the tendency to remember the first and last information presented to us in a series. Want to know how powerful the primacy effect is? What are two things I just mentioned about myself?

Yes, I am a father, and yes, I am a doctor. But if you were to ask me who I am and what I do, I would tell you I am a "global lifestyle architect." I guide and motivate others to define their "Why" in order to design and thrive in the lifestyle of their choice. I do this by introducing them to five simple steps to get the results they want in their lives.

First, we identify the vision of the desired life. From there, we determine their mission in that life. Once we have those, we set some critical objective milestones to meet. Together, we strategize their smart goals. Finally, we execute action steps to get results! This five-step "Lifestyle Blueprint" has been implemented for hundreds of my clients, and I'm proud to say everyone who has gone through this program has met their goals annually! That's one-hundred percent guaranteed results because it revolves around one critical part of every neoprenuer—their Why.

When we live our lives only focusing on "what" it is we want to do, we meet a very frustrating end result. We are multi-talented—born that way. Even a baby is great at, at least, three things: eat, sleep, cry. By focusing on the What, you will immediately be typecast into the person you don't want to be.

Before his untimely passing, Chadwick Boseman made it clear how he never wanted to compromise himself by acting in roles that he felt did not improve his community. Because he understood his Why and wouldn't allow himself to settle, Chadwick declined roles that depicted him as a slave and even got fired from roles that portrayed him as a son of a crackhead mother. He then strategized on what roles to take.

As his reputation grew, so did his value. In 2016, Chadwick received a call, based on his lifelong mission to improve the condition of humanity, to play T'Challa in the Marvel Studios movie *Black Panther*—a movie that would hit a record-breaking $1 billion in box offices worldwide. He also hit a major milestone in changing how children around the world see superheroes.

Imagine what this world would've missed out on if this neo-prenuer didn't make decisions based on his Why. Imagine what the world is missing if you allow your life to be defined by what you do, rather than why you do it. When we are faced with the Why, the What and the How become endless. The question of "What do I want to do for the rest of my life," instead of causing pain and anguish, will exhilarate, motivate, and propel you to create a meaningful lifestyle that allows you to thrive.

Moreover, when we are defined by the Why, everything we do will be great. This is why the title of this chapter is "Ace of All Trades." When focusing on the Why, everything we do is geared toward creating the vision we will create. What happens afterward is a result of enacting those five simple steps in the "Lifestyle Blueprint."

So, what will you do next? As a neo-prenuer, you're calculating the risk of progressing forward with defining your Why. You're asking yourself if it is even possible at this time to reflect on years of self-development and dive deeper to identify your Why. Do you have the time? And if it took this long to learn the lesson of how truly powerful not knowing the Why is, then can you afford to waste any more time without it?

Imagine yourself as an "intrapreneur," going to work every day to help a large corporation become even greater than before. Imagine being overlooked for that promotion you've been trying to claim. Was it because what you did wasn't good enough or because no one knew why you wanted to move up in the company and how truly great that would be for everyone if you achieved your Why?

Imagine yourself as an entrepreneur, looking to create a new marketing and branding kit for this amazing new product you have. You post it on Instagram; you explain all of its features; you share it on Twitter and Facebook; and yet no one even likes the post. Well, no one except your mom believes in you, and she knows how hard and why this is so important to you. But does your audience know?

When you use the "Lifestyle Blueprint" and effectively answer every section, you will find that the results you are looking for are just byproducts of why you are doing what you are doing. Not only will it change your ability to secure stable capital, financial freedom, but you will have a lifestyle that you can be proud of. To truly thrive is to produce results that are meaningful enough to bring joy to your life and those around you.

I am offering a free copy of the "Lifestyle Blueprint." I want you to take advantage of being a great neo-prenuer and utilize all the talents you possess; that is:

- A neo-prenuer who stands out at work
- A neo-prenuer who is an effective leader.
- A neo-prenuer who impresses their clients with genuine products and services
- A neo-prenuer who is confident and happy with who they are.

Together let's thrive in prosperity and happiness. Stay Well!

– Your Global Lifestyle Architect (The Ace of All Trades)

Dr. Glenn T. Miller: Ace of All Trades

Dr. Glenn T. Miller is a lifestyle coach and wellness doctor. With a doctorate in chiropractic and certificates as a life coach, lifestyle expert, and small business consultant, he has spent the past decade as a full-time entrepreneur, helping others create their ideal lifestyles. Dr. Miller graduated from Logan University, where he received an award for diversity and inclusion for his work in creating inclusive organizations.

Dr. Miller is a member of Alpha Phi Alpha Fraternity, Inc., and 100 Black Men of St. Louis, both organizations geared toward advancing the community through leadership, education, and economic empowerment.

Dr. Miller's mission is to facilitate the experience of living an optimal lifestyle for all to operate and thrive in, to build relationships across his diverse community, to help others discover, dream, plan, and implement platforms of success and equip them with the tools needed to be community and global citizens.

Info@IAmDrWellness.com
linktr.ee/IAmDrWellness
iamdrwellness.com

ROB WHITMAN

For Sale by Owner

Are you planning on moving and interested in saving thousands of dollars? Are you concerned about getting your home ready to list, show, and sell? Well, here is my story and tips to make your journey easy and profitable.

It was early February 2018. My wife, Connie, and I have two sons who were both in college and our bills were starting to grow. Connie and I had been kicking around the idea of downsizing our home to save money to help pay off the college debt. We realized that, after living in our home for more than twenty-five years, things were starting to wear out and we would need to update things such as the deck and air-conditioning system. We also knew that these were expenses and not investments in our home that would increase its value.

So we began to look at homes that we felt would suit our needs. One day, there was an open house in a townhouse development in the next town. We decided to take a look to see if we could envision living in a townhouse. After touring it, we instantly knew that this was a place that had enough room for our needs. We could also envision ourselves happily living there. We were certainly not ready to make a move like this, but we put the offer in anyway. We did this without having done a single thing to prepare our home to be listed for sale. Looking back, we were fortunate that our offer wasn't accepted because we had a lot of work to do before we were ready to sell our house. With that said, we knew we needed to get our house ready to sell so we would be prepared to put an offer in when another townhouse came on the market.

We weighed the pros and cons of using a Realtor and ultimately decided that we wanted to take a shot at selling our home ourselves. Our game plan was to give ourselves one month to sell and if we weren't successful, we would ask a good friend of ours, who is a Realtor, to list our house for sale.

Knowing that springtime is usually a good time to try to sell a house, we knew that we had to move fast. We decided to change our winter vacation plans to take a long weekend to visit friends in Florida. Instead, we rolled up our sleeves to get the house ready.

We figured that we had watched enough HGTV to give us some direction, but we also realized that HGTV programs are just TV shows and not reality. I wanted to make sure that we had as few blind spots as possible, so I started to research how to sell a house without a Realtor. I scoured the Internet for information, as well as asked our Realtor friends questions. After completing my research and discussing it with Connie, we came up with a plan. The plan consisted of three phases: 1) prepare the house, 2) price and list the house, and 3) show and close the house.

Phase 1

This phase needs to be done whether or not you are using a Realtor. This is the phase that includes making any necessary repairs and improvements (both inside and outside) that helps the house show better. Thankfully, the outside of our house was cleaned up and would show well. This allowed us to focus on the inside. We decided to divide and concur our tasks. Connie took on the role of decluttering and depersonalizing the house, and I took on the responsibility of painting and making any necessary repairs. The next weekend, instead of relaxing in the Florida sun, we put in twelve-plus-hour days to get everything done. I replaced some light fixtures, fixed a leaky faucet, and painted the three bedrooms, hallway, and foyer.

Connie started by removing anything extra that would make the house look cluttered. Our objective was to try to make the house look like a model home that you would see in a magazine. This meant that there were very few pictures of our family (we had a lot of pictures), and any unnecessary furniture was removed and put into storage to help the house feel more spacious. The goal was to make it as easy as possible for potential buyers to envision their belongings in our house.

Tip: You want potential buyers to look at the house as their home and not see it as someone else's home. To me, it seems kind of silly, but everyone's mind, feelings, and emotions are different, so who am I to judge.

All in, it took us about three weeks to get the house ready.

Phase 2

We decided to list our home on Zillow, which is a public website for selling homes. Before doing that, we had to determine the sale price to list the house, write a description for the listing, and take pictures to post on the website. Pricing was probably the most nerve-racking part of the process as this would be the starting point for any negotiations.

We conducted a thorough market analysis to determine what we believed was the fair market value based on recent comparable sales. We were of the opinion that, if we were not using a Realtor, a benefit to the buyer would be that we would split the savings of the Realtor's commissions.

I reviewed online descriptions of other listings of similar homes and wrote a draft. I had it reviewed by Connie to make sure it made sense and didn't have any typos. We felt it was important to have a professional real estate photographer take the house photos, using the proper camera lens and lightening. This was another great decision. The photos looked professional and the images on the Zillow website looked amazing. The pictures were well worth the $130 spent.

Listing a house on Zillow couldn't have been easier. It was just a matter of following the steps and answering their questions.

Tip: Ask the photographer to provide a list of things to do to prepare for the photo shoot.

Phase 3

We put a "For Sale by Owner" sign on our front lawn and activated the listing on Zillow on a Thursday; we held an open house that next Sunday. We cleaned and scrubbed the house from top to bottom to get it ready. We were shocked at the number of Realtors that contacted us asking if they could list our house. Other Realtors asked, if they had a potential buyer, if we were open to working with them. This was something that we weren't expecting; but we agreed and were up front with them that they would need to work their commission out directly with their homebuyer/client.

Within a week, we had a couple of people interested in the house and we negotiated a contract with one of them. As it turned out, the couple who we sold the house to was using a Realtor. This did make the contract portion a bit easier as the Realtor had the real estate agency's standard offering contract. We handled the initial back-and-forth negotiations, then once the attorney review was complete, the attorneys took over the remaining back-and-forth communications. Our attorney walked us through the process all the way to the closing.

Looking back, selling our home without a Realtor was the right move for us. In the end, we also decided to buy our new townhouse without a Realtor. The breakdown of savings for us by selling the house ourselves was about $25,000; buying a house, negotiating directly with the seller of our current townhouse saved us another $20,000.

Yes, there were a couple of obstacles that we didn't anticipate, but overall, it was a relatively smooth process. It took us some research and planning, but the amount of effort wasn't a whole lot more than if we were to list the house with a Realtor.

> **Tip:** Selling a house without a Realtor isn't for everyone, but if you're considering it, I encourage you to give it a try. You can always hire a Realtor at a later date if it doesn't work out.

Rob Whitman was born and raised in Ontario, Canada, and immigrated with his family to the United States when he was twelve years old.

Rob has over thirty years of experience in the financial services industry, helping financial advisors understand complex retirement-planning concepts. He has developed many technical training programs that have helped provide a sound foundation for new advisors' careers. In addition, he has five years of experience following his passion of investing in real estate and founded Your Town Properties LLC. He has focused on buying and selling houses in Ohio, New York, and New Jersey.

Rob currently lives in New Jersey with his wife, Connie, and his two sons.

ytprop@yahoo.com
www.linkedin.com/in/rob-whitman-5a26b062

KIMBERLY WEITKAMP

Avoiding Marketing Free Fall

I was suspended over a snow-covered valley in a simple harness with only a piece of rope anchoring me. The wooden platform I'd stepped off moments before was just out of arm's reach. The cold air whipped past me as the snow from the recent blizzard stung my face. All that stood between me and free fall was a single cord holding me to a suspension line.

I closed my eyes…and pulled the cord.

My screams of delight and fear were lost in the whipping wind as I swung across the valley in Queenstown, New Zealand. The forty-five-second pendulum swing seemed to last an eternity. Every moment, I thought I was a second away from crashing into the prickly fir trees below.

This bungee activity is considered one of the most difficult in New Zealand. Not because it's the tallest. Not because it's the most unique location. Unlike other bungee activities, YOU have to take the final leap. No one can push you off the platform or nudge you. The operators can't pull the cord to start the free fall; you have to do it yourself.

This was a transformative experience for me. I had been contemplating creating and starting my own copywriting business for months. I was living in a foreign country, far from home, traveling on a tour bus for months with no solid base. I didn't know if I had what it would take to build my own business.

I decided that if I could yank the cord, rely on a single harness to support me and keep me alive, starting a business couldn't be THAT scary.

The Support Needed for Marketing

I found that singular experience prepared me for working with my best clients, too.

Many people I work with describe marketing like "falling off a cliff." They feel like they have no control; they're scared of what comes next; and they don't know if they have the right supports in place.

As someone who voluntarily swung from a cliff, I know that personal feeling well.

The clients I work with often put together launches. For those who don't know, a "launch" is simply a specific period of time when a company makes a service or course available for purchase online. Usually, the period can last three to four weeks, and it's very elaborate. There are a lot of moving pieces, and it can be a very scary time for business owners.

For many of them, it feels like going into a launch is similar to being in free fall…except it lasts months instead of sixty seconds. They're waiting for that cord to rip free. They're worried about what will happen once they take that leap and rip the cord away on the first day of their promotion. Once they release themselves over the mountainside, they lose complete control of the process, and it can be scary.

And that is where I come in.

I'm the guide…the harness…the support they need to enjoy the ride so they can shout with glee, instead of terror, and get to where they need to go.

One of my clients really embodies this story.

The Go-It-Alone Approach

Dave was doing his very first launch. He'd seen other people put on successful launches and thought he could do it himself. He gathered all his materials and started creating his campaign…the emails…the landing pages…the sales page…the webinar. It's a lot of moving pieces, and he felt he could reach his goals on his own. He felt he was in control.

Only three weeks before his launch date, that feeling of free fall and doubt increased. He began to feel out of control. He wanted a "harness" to support him before he took that leap. He searched for an expert to give his launch that final touch and feedback. He reached out to me.

As the date his promotion would go live was only a few weeks away, I asked for all of the materials he'd already finished to take an initial look. During that first call, I noticed he was missing a piece of his support system.

You Don't Know What You Don't Know

Often, as business owners and entrepreneurs who are passionate about what we do, we're too close to see the small things that are missing. We excel at what we're good at, but we overlook or miss the simple things. My clients are focused on the value they'll be giving to their audience and not on all the details of their marketing campaign.

After reviewing Dave's materials, I asked a single question that made all the difference: "Do you have a cart-close email?"

I got a blank stare in return.

When we take the "I can do it myself" mentality, we don't know what we don't know. Dave didn't know what a cart-close email was, much less the value it could bring to his campaign. He was suspended over the valley of his launch and didn't know he would crash without the missing piece of support.

A Fifty-Percent Bump in Sales

People aren't motivated to take action until the opportunity is almost gone. A cart-close email is a series of emails you send on the final day you're offering your product or service to remind people about the sale. Up to fifty percent of sales come on the last day.

True to my prediction, half of Dave's sales came on the final day. These sales were direct clicks from the cart-close emails. I have been working with Dave on every single one of his campaigns since.

Marketing Doesn't Need to Be a Cliff Jump

Marketing doesn't have to be a big, scary jump-off-a-cliff moment. It doesn't need to be a dive into the unknown.

Right before I pulled the cord for my bungee swing, the operator pointed to one part of the harness and said, "Don't touch this. It's what's keeping you safe." After the cord is pulled, you want to hang on to something. But the only part of the harness that sticks out is the one thing you're not supposed to touch.

After my first jump, I did something even crazier. I signed up to jump again… later that same day. The bungee company offered a ridiculously cheap upgrade if you wanted to jump twice in one day. I'd seen the city in the day and thought it would be nice to see the view of the valley at night. Oddly enough, I was more scared the second time around. I knew what to expect.

This time, I really wanted somewhere I could hang on, so I asked the operator. He advised, "Grab the shoulder straps of the harness and hang on to yourself."

It took an extra fifteen minutes suspended over the valley before I was ready to pull that cord again. All of the old fears seemed to double, and I was worried about relying solely on myself and the harness.

Luckily, in the world of marketing, you don't need to just rely on yourself. You can rely on outsiders and experts who know exactly what they are doing: experts who can give you more handholds than yourself and be far enough away from your company to give you the right outsider's perspective. It's easy to tell someone to "pull the cord" when you've seen thousands of people achieve it safely. You're far enough removed.

Unlike the person in the harness.

For many people, marketing, especially creating a campaign for a large launch, can feel like pushing off the edge of a cliff. And it doesn't have to be that way.

Find someone who can support you throughout the process…to be your own harness: the trusted operator who can explain things to you and be a partner along the way, not an order-taker.

When I worked with Dave the first time, we discussed his goals, went over his preparations, and answered several questions about the process, which led to questions he hadn't thought to ask before.

When I work with a client, it's not just about the words. We jump on calls. We talk through the technology. I act not only as the writer and the outside support during the process; I also act as advisor, mentor, and guide.

None of my clients need to jump off the cliff alone. I'm there to help them… and it makes all the difference.

Kimberly Weitkamp is a marketing strategist, podcaster, and conversion copywriter. She's based in St. Louis, Missouri, and serves an international clientele.

Kimberly developed the *Audience Conversion Method* to help coaches and consultants convert their audience from strangers to loyal fans. She brings this work to an international audience with her company, The Audience Converter, and as host of the *Audience Converter Podcast for Community Leaders*.

As an AWAI-verified direct-response copywriter, Kimberly works with her clients to attract, build, and grow an engaged audience and community to create long-term customers. She specializes in emails, landing pages, and sales pages that convert.

Kimberly has helped people increase their open rate up to eighty percent, hit their first-ever six-figure launch, and double conversions on their landing pages. She loves talking marketing, travel, and all things sci-fi.

When she's not working with her clients, she loves to travel and go dancing.

contact@theaudienceconverter.com
theaudienceconverter.com
www.linkedin.com/in/kimberlyweitkamp/
www.facebook.com/audienceconverter/
www.instagram.com/audienceconverter/
www.twitter.com/k_weitkamp
636-614-2217

JOANNE WEILAND

Go for the Green

Imagine the energy of a thousand people attending the world renowned "Speak and Grow Rich," four-day, intensive conference, held in the midst of a cold winter month in sunny Florida. What happened there was almost unbelievable!

Unbeknownst to each, four former comrades were attending the same conference. Connie was shocked when she saw Sam at the snack bar; Willie was thrilled when he was behind Nancy in the lunch line; Nancy and Connie were delighted to find themselves in the same ladies' room during a break.

Five years earlier, each having spent ten-plus years in the industry, these four seasoned co-workers communicated often, sharing ideas, frustrations, and wins on their weekly sales and marketing calls. Unfortunately, they had lost track of each other.

When Nancy saw Connie, she told her she had run into Willie.

"Your kidding?" Connie said. "Sam is here too!"

Well, that calls for a reunion, the ladies agreed.

Connie, the "Connector," scheduled a get-together for drinks after the last session of the day.

In the hotel lounge, they embraced, laughed, and shared what had been happening in their lives for the past half decade. Sam had moved to St. Louis; Willie was still in DC; Nancy was temporarily in Colorado; Connie was grateful to be in Florida and out of the New Jersey cold.

The foursome reminisced about working in corporate America and competing against undercutting rivals; they also recalled competing against each other in meeting monthly sales goals.

Willie said, "Remember when we created a contest between us to see who could reach six figures first within twelve months!"

Sam said softly, "Yes, we made games to ease the stress."

"Since then, we all have been laid off, downsized, right-sized, or left to 'be our own bosses,'" said Nancy. "None of us ever reached $100K!"

"Yes," Connie spoke up. "I did in 2012! The Bradley deal closed after I had stayed in touch through their mergers and acquisitions. Have any of you reached $100K on your own?"

No, no, and no, they all said shaking their heads.

Then came a stream of reasons why they had not been able to enjoy the benefits of being a $100K entrepreneur:

- I never liked cold calling.
- I hate going to useless networking meetings.
- I spend a lot of my time on proposals and never hear back from prospective clients.
- Social media sucks; it takes too much time.
- I would follow up if I had a client relationship management (CRM) package.
- I have lots of ideas but I get distracted and don't know how to monetize them.

"What if we create a new competition," Willie said. "Call it, 'Go for the green.'"

Throughout the conference, this group of four had learned conventional wisdom from many well-known experts. Willie summarized the top five insights of becoming a successful entrepreneur:

1. Create products and services/active, passive, and residual income.
2. Build a website.
3. Network, network, network—continually build your list.
4. Create alliances/partnerships/joint ventures with colleagues/affiliates/vendors.
5. Be seen on stages. Be heard in interviews. Be known as the "expert."

Okay. Game on! They agreed and planned to meet on Zoom in 120 days to review their progress.

Sam, the introvert of the group, moved into a downtown skyscraper. He was proud to get his name and company's name on the marque for all to see. He built alliances with the tenants in the building without having to interact with them—except on the elevator!

Nancy decided to build her list and became known as the "Networking Queen." Sometimes she participated in three networking meetings per day, paying catering charges of $20 to $150 for each. She collected several hundred business cards over those few months.

Willie followed the advice of a conference expert who had said to create a website that includes a blog, interviews, video presentations, and an online store. For the next ninety days, he worked with web developers, designers, and programmers to create his own website. After doing all that, he was surprised he wasn't getting many visitors.

Connie, as the Connector, decided to join a collaborative cloud community. She moved into her own website in just a few hours. Every week she created new blogs, videos, electronic products, and services which were distributed to the database of executives, entrepreneurs, event professionals, experts, and media. Her messages reached tens of thousands of decision-makers on social media platforms, like Twitter, Facebook, and LinkedIn. She was interviewed in more publications, and on more radio and podcast shows in four months than she had been in five years. She was in the limelight, being seen, heard, and known as the expert by spending five minutes a week at a fraction of the cost it would take to do it herself. Additionally, the community elevated her reputation as the expert in her field. She was winning awards to confirm it. The most exciting part was she could focus on what she loved and did best!

Who do you think was the first to reach the green? Is it time for **YOU** to go for the green?

Note from the Author (the "Connector")

I hope you enjoyed my almost true story that reflects what I experienced when transitioning from a corporate job to becoming an entrepreneur. It takes courage to go out on your own and leave the comfort of a paycheck—or worse, get thrown out of the nest by being laid off, downsized, or right-sized.

You might feel worthless for some time, like I did. Don't worry. It is part of the process.

It is scary entering the unknown. You will encounter issues and will hear some of the same advice we heard at the conference. But conventional wisdom has its own problems. I have solutions:

Conventional Wisdom #1: Create products and services/active, passive, and residual income.

- *Challenge:* "I was always told to diversify but I remained stuck with one stream of income." "I never liked cold calling." "I have lots of ideas but I get distracted and don't know how to monetize them."
- *Solution:* Create products and services that produce a stream of income. Develop active, passive, and residual income by working with ghost writers, publishers, and editors in creating books, white papers, e-tips, and/or e-courses.

Conventional Wisdom #2: Build a website.

- *Challenge:* "I was embarrassed to send prospective clients to my homemade website; it looked like a third-grader made it." "I would follow up if I had a CRM package."
- *Solution:* Hire experts to build a professional-looking website you are proud to claim and where your blogs, videos, podcasts, radio interviews, products, and services are in one place. Build in the ability to manage your emails and regular contacts with clients to maintain your rapport.

Conventional Wisdom #3: Network, network, network—continually build your list.

- *Challenge:* "I hate going to useless networking meetings." "Occasionally, I would send out a newsletter to about 350 of the contacts I met at networking meetings."
- *Solution:* Consider being featured in a newsletter amongst other experts, which is automatically distributed to your own list of customers and tens of thousands of prospective. Caveat: Keep your database updated; it is your goldmine.

Conventional Wisdom #4: Create alliances/partnerships/joint ventures with colleagues/affiliates/vendors.
- *Challenge:* "I have been told about the value of forming alliances, joint ventures, of becoming affiliates with colleagues and vendors. But I never found the time to make it a reality." "I spend a lot of my time on proposals and never hear back from prospective clients." "Social media sucks; it takes too much time."
- *Solution:* Fortunately, extraordinary experts, affiliates, and vendors who want to work together on projects, form alliances, and make money together are members of the collaborative cloud community.

Conventional Wisdom #5: Be seen on stages. Be heard in interviews. Be known as the "expert."
- *Challenge:* "I felt like an imposter (Who do I think I am? The authority?)."
- *Solution:* The collaborative cloud community creates alliances/partnerships with the media—radio show hosts, podcasters, newswires, publications to showcase you, which elevates your status to be known as the expert worldwide. These organizations have access to networks of executives, entrepreneurs, event professionals, experts, and the media, all wanting to collaborate.

In essence, there are easier ways for you to go for the green. And the "Connector" created them!

Along with the above, have faith in yourself, take action to do what you love and live the life of your dreams. I dare you.

Continued…

Joanne Weiland invents industries. She is the founder of LinktoEXPERT Collaboration Cloud Community, which connects executives, entrepreneurs, event professionals, and the media worldwide. LinktoEXPERT assists clients in taking their businesses online, securing more speaking engagements, and creating more streams of income. Through Collaboration Cloud Community, clients can find an expert, review their credentials, and hire them in minutes.

Members of this online community create their messages; and LinktoEXPERT, with its unique database exchange program, distributes them to decision-makers all over the world.

Joanne persistently networks, building relationships and joint ventures. She is continually interviewed on podcasts and radio shows worldwide and was a "growth hacker" before she knew that measuring marketing results was growth hacking.

Joanne encourages everyone to be all they are designed to be. Be seen. Be heard. Be known worldwide with ease!

jweiland@LinktoEXPERT.com
www.LinktoEXPERT.com
www.JoanneWeiland.LinktoEXPERT.com
www.linkedin.com/in/jweiland
www.facebook.com/LinktoEXPERT
twitter.com/LinktoEXPERT
www.youtube.com/mylinktoexpert
727.791.7338 phone
727.243.9453 text

MEREDITH MCVEHIL

Sleepless to Hopeful about Money

Losing with money? Are you tossing and turning at night because of money worries? Are the bills and debts piling up and keeping you distracted at work and at home? Do you wonder if you are saving enough for retirement, kids' college, or another emergency? Well, I am here to tell you that there IS hope! There IS a way to end the crazy cycle of worry and stress when it comes to personal finances!

The struggle is real.

Years ago, my former husband and I ran a small business together and struggled to make ends meet. Sleepless nights worrying, pouring over the numbers, and stressing out about money was my *norm* every single day. With two young boys under the age of five, a home, constant fights, and worry, we "invested" (borrowed the money) to purchase a small house in the north county area of St. Louis in late 2007 thinking that making it into a rental property would help our cash flow. We opened a Home Depot credit card, bought needed supplies, and ran up $30,000 in credit card debt. Thanks to the market crash of 2008, we ended up with a mountain of debt we couldn't pay off, a higher pile of money worries, fears, and fights! In a moment of panic, I signed up for Dave Ramsey's Financial Peace University nine-week course at our church. In class, we learned how to budget, save for emergencies, wipe out our debts with intensity, and to live within our means going forward. *We paid off $30,000 in less than two years applying the principles we had learned through Dave Ramsey.*

Although that marriage ended in divorce, the lessons of that class stayed with me. A single mom of two young boys, I was able to cash-flow our lives, live in our home, and stay on a budget without any more debt!

Wait! Things get even better! In 2016, I married my best friend and love of my life: Jeff. He came to our marriage with $200,000 of debt including sixteen credit cards and a second mortgage. Yes, you read that correctly: $200,000 of DEBT! Implementing the principles as before, Jeff and I got on the same page with money, worked out monthly budgets TOGETHER, and in February of 2018, just short of twenty-four months, paid off all of that nasty debt! In fact, in December of 2020 we paid off our home mortgage, crushing more than $600,000 in debt in four years! Naturally, this fueled my passion for teaching others how to live on a budget and become debt free, so I became a Ramsey Preferred Money Coach! To date, between family, friends, and clients, I have guided others to pay off more than *$1 million in debt.*

The Dreaded "B" Word

Did you know that personal finance is eighty percent BEHAVIOR and twenty percent knowledge? You MUST start with a budget, also known as a "cash flow plan," giving every one of your incoming dollars an assignment. Instead of asking at the end of the month "Where does all of the money go?" when you create a budget, you tell your dollars where to go, make your money behave, and give each dollar direction and a purpose.

TIP: Everything about money is learning to control your behavior.

Budget to Zero Before the Month Begins

This means before the month even starts, you're making a plan and giving every dollar a name. It's called a "zero-based budget." Now, that doesn't mean you have zero dollars in your bank account. It just means your income minus all your expenses (outgo) equals zero. If you're married, do the budget together. If the two of you are one, your bank accounts should be one too! It's no longer *your* money or *my* money—it's *our* money.

And if you're single, find someone who can act as your accountability partner and help you stick to your goals like a best friend or money coach.

Every month is different. Some months you'll have to budget for things like back-to-school supplies or routine car maintenance. Other months, you'll be saving for things like vacations, birthdays, and holidays. Regardless of the occasion, make sure you prepare for those expenses in the budget. Don't let these special occasions sneak up on you. Hint: Christmas is in December again this year, so create a gift fund where you can stash cash throughout the year. That way you have a plan and can give with joy without the stress of more debt!

TIP: Create a separate savings account of $1,000 cash for basic emergencies and for irregular expenses, like HOA dues, gifts, and car repairs.

Start with the Most Important Categories First

Giving and saving are at the top of the list and then comes the "four walls"—food, shelter and utilities, basic clothing, and transportation. Once your *true* necessities are taken care of, you can fill in the rest of the categories in your budget. These are key areas to pay first so you don't run the risk of foreclosure or having creditors call you about the lights or the water or your car.

Pay Off Your Debt

If you have debt, paying it off needs to be a top priority. Use the "debt snowball method" to get rid of debt as fast as you can. Attack it! Get mad at it! Stop letting debt rob you of the very thing that helps you win with money—your income.

TIP: List ALL debts (excluding the mortgage) including medical bills, from smallest to largest, ignoring the interest rates. Pay off the smallest amount due first and build momentum from there.

Don't Be Afraid To Trim the Budget

Brace yourself! It might be time for some budget cuts in your life. If things are tight right now, you can save money quickly by canceling your cable, dining out less, and shopping at discount clothing and grocery stores.

TIP: One key category to keep a close eye on is your grocery budget. You will spend less on groceries on a budget. Food, to include restaurants, should add up to no more than 10-15% of your take home pay. Contact me for a handy guide to help you budget for groceries.

Create A Buffer in Your Budget

Put a small amount of money aside for unexpected expenses throughout the month. Label this as a miscellaneous category in your budget. That way when something comes up, you can cover it without taking away money you've already put somewhere else. Keep track of expenses that frequently end up in this category. Eventually, you might even want to promote them to a permanent spot on the budget roster.

Cut Up Your Credit Cards

If you're committed to sticking to a budget and getting out of debt, you need to ditch those credit cards for good. Stop using them! Cut them up, shred them, or even make a craft project out of them! Whatever you do—get them out of your life.

Having no credit card debt will mean no more minimum payments to add to the budget, zero hassle with fees or high interest rates, and much less stress and worry! Stick to using your debit card (and even cash!) and dump those credit cards NOW.

TIP: Debt is dumb and cash is king!

Use cash

If you're constantly overspending on your grocery budget or fun money, cash out those categories and use the envelope system to hold you accountable. Just go to the bank and pull out the cash amount you've budgeted for that category. Once the cash runs out, stop spending! It's the ultimate accountability partner.

Try an Online Budget Tool

If pen and paper (or spreadsheets) aren't your thing, it's time to join the twenty-first century and use a budgeting tool like EveryDollar.com. You can focus on planning a budget and tracking your spending from the comfort of your smartphone! Plus, you can sync up your budget with your spouse, which is great for keeping communication open.

Give Yourself Grace

It takes three to four months to get this budgeting practice figured out. Please remember to give you and your spouse (if applicable) lots of grace. Like any new habit, it takes time and discipline, and there is a learning curve. However, once the budgeting habit becomes second nature, you will feel peace, get more sleep, and know you are winning with money.

Meredith McVehil is a Ramsey Preferred Money Coach in the St. Louis area. She is passionate about coaching individuals and families to a life of financial peace and freedom. After eliminating her family's debt, Meredith discovered her newfound love of coaching others on how to win with money. To date, she has helped others crush one million dollars in debt!

Originally from St. Louis, Meredith spent four years in Chicago working in public relations. She returned to St. Louis and served as the marketing director for one of the area's largest home builders, becoming an award-winning new home sales professional. Additionally, she co-owned a business and spear-headed the growth of a local title company's West County office.

In addition to being a money coach, Meredith is a wife, mother of two high-school young men, bonus mom to two, "GiGi" to her granddaughter, two-time breast cancer survivor, and proud owner of Ace, an energetic eighty-five-pound puppy.

314-724-1043
mmcvehilpeace@gmail.com
Follow her on FB at "Merediths Money Matters"

Right now, the world needs us to…

Be Nice
Be Kind
Be Safe
Take Care of Each Other
SHINE

If you, or someone you know, would like to submit
a chapter in one of our upcoming compilation anthologies,
please visit daviscreative.com/anthology-services

www.ingramcontent.com/pod-product-compliance
Lightning Source LLC
LaVergne TN
LVHW011853060526
838200LV00054B/4304